IT'S TIME TO EAT CLEMENTINES

It's Time to Eat CLEMENTINES

Walter the Educator

Silent King Books
A WhichHead Entertainment Imprint

Copyright © 2024 by Walter the Educator

All rights reserved. No part of this book may be reproduced in any manner whatsoever without written per- mission except in the case of brief quotations embodied in critical articles and reviews.

First Printing, 2024

Disclaimer

This book is a literary work; the story is not about specific persons, locations, situations, and/or circumstances unless mentioned in a historical context. Any resemblance to real persons, locations, situations, and/or circumstances is coincidental. This book is for entertainment and informational purposes only. The author and publisher offer this information without warranties expressed or implied. No matter the grounds, neither the author nor the publisher will be accountable for any losses, injuries, or other damages caused by the reader's use of this book. The use of this book acknowledges an understanding and acceptance of this disclaimer.

It's Time to Eat CLEMENTINES is a collectible early learning book by Walter the Educator suitable for all ages belonging to Walter the Educator's Time to Eat Book Series. Collect more books at WaltertheEducator.com

USE THE EXTRA SPACE TO TAKE NOTES AND DOCUMENT YOUR MEMORIES

CLEMENTINES

It's time to eat, hooray, hooray!

It's Time to Eat
Clementines

A clementine will make your day.

Orange and round, so full of cheer,

A perfect snack is waiting here.

Peel the skin, it comes off quick,

Easy to open, just take your pick!

Inside are slices, small and neat,

A juicy fruit that's fun to eat.

They're sweet and tangy, such a treat,

Soft and tender, not too sweet.

With every bite, you'll surely find,

A burst of sunshine, oh so kind!

Packed with vitamin C galore,

Clementines help you feel strong and more.

They keep you healthy, bright, and glad,

A better snack can't be had!

It's Time to Eat
Clementines

For lunch or breakfast, any time,

They're always fresh, they're always prime.

At home, at school, or on the go,

Clementines are the way to glow!

No sticky mess, they're easy to share,

Hand them out, show that you care.

With friends or family, pass them around,

Happiness in each slice is found.

They grow on trees with leaves so green,

In sunny orchards, they can be seen.

Picked with care, and sent to you,

A fruit that's special through and through.

Little seeds may hide inside,

But don't let that hurt your stride.

Just pick them out, it's worth the fun,

It's Time to Eat
Clementines

And keep on eating, one by one.

So grab a clementine today,

It's time to snack the tasty way.

Orange and round, so sweet and fine,

The perfect snack, your clementine!

When hunger calls and you must dine,

Think of this fruity friend of mine.

Healthy, yummy, and oh so bright,

It's Time to Eat
Clementines

Clementines make everything just right!

ABOUT THE CREATOR

Walter the Educator is one of the pseudonyms for Walter Anderson. Formally educated in Chemistry, Business, and Education, he is an educator, an author, a diverse entrepreneur, and he is the son of a disabled war veteran. "Walter the Educator" shares his time between educating and creating. He holds interests and owns several creative projects that entertain, enlighten, enhance, and educate, hoping to inspire and motivate you. Follow, find new works, and stay up to date with Walter the Educator™

at WaltertheEducator.com

www.ingramcontent.com/pod-product-compliance
Lightning Source LLC
LaVergne TN
LVHW052011060526
838201LV00059B/3971